The 2014 Military Op Gaza in Response to Attacks by Hamas

Copyright Page

TITLE: The 2014 Israeli Military Operation in Gaza in Response to Attacks by Hamas

1ST Edition

Table of Contents

The 2014 Israeli Military Operation in Gaza in Response to Attacks by Hamas

By Roberto Miguel Rodriguez

Chapter 1: Operation Protective Edge: The 2014 Israeli Military Operation in Gaza in Response to Rocket Attacks by Hamas

Background of the Israeli-Palestinian Conflict

The Israeli-Palestinian conflict is a complex and deeply rooted issue that has plagued the Middle East for decades. In order to fully understand the context of Operation Protective Edge, it is essential to explore the historical background of this conflict.

The roots of the Israeli-Palestinian conflict can be traced back to the late 19th century, when Zionist Jews began to immigrate to Palestine with the aim of establishing a Jewish homeland. This wave of Jewish immigration was met with resistance from the Arab population, who feared losing their land and national identity.

Tensions between Jews and Arabs escalated in the early 20th century, leading to sporadic violence and clashes. The conflict reached a climax in 1947 when the United Nations proposed the partition of Palestine into separate Jewish and Arab states. The Jewish community accepted this proposal, but the Arab states rejected it, sparking a full-scale war.

The 1948 Arab-Israeli War resulted in the establishment of the State of Israel and the displacement of hundreds of thousands of Palestinian Arabs, who became refugees in neighboring countries. This event, known as the Nakba or "Catastrophe," remains a deeply divisive issue to this day.

Since then, the Israeli-Palestinian conflict has been characterized by a series of wars, uprisings, and peace processes. The issues at the heart of the conflict include the status of Jerusalem, the borders of Israel, the right of return for Palestinian refugees, and the establishment of a Palestinian state.

Operation Protective Edge, the 2014 Israeli military operation in Gaza, was a direct response to rocket attacks launched by Hamas, the Islamist political and military organization governing the Gaza Strip. This operation further exacerbated the already tense Israeli-Palestinian relations and had wide-ranging consequences.

Understanding the historical background of the Israeli-Palestinian conflict is crucial for historians and politicians alike. It provides the necessary context to analyze the motivations and actions of the parties involved. By examining the roots of the conflict, it becomes evident that there is no easy solution and that any attempt at peace must take into account the deep-seated grievances and aspirations of both Israelis and Palestinians.

This subchapter aims to provide a comprehensive overview of the historical background of the Israeli-Palestinian conflict, setting the stage for a deeper analysis of Operation Protective Edge and its long-term implications. By understanding the complexities of this conflict, historians and politicians can gain valuable insights into the factors that have shaped and continue to shape the Israeli-Palestinian relationship.

Rise of Hamas in Gaza and Rocket Attacks on Israel

The subchapter "Rise of Hamas in Gaza and Rocket Attacks on Israel" delves into the historical background and political context that led to the rise of Hamas as a dominant force in Gaza and the subsequent rocket attacks on Israel. This subchapter aims to provide historians and politicians with a comprehensive understanding of the events surrounding Operation Protective Edge and its implications for both the Israeli-Palestinian conflict and the wider international community.

The rise of Hamas in Gaza can be traced back to the Israeli occupation and subsequent disengagement from the Gaza Strip in 2005. With the absence of Israeli control, Hamas capitalized on the vacuum of power and emerged as a formidable political and military force. The subchapter explores the factors that contributed to the popularity of Hamas, including its extensive social welfare programs and its opposition to the perceived corruption of the Palestinian Authority.

The rocket attacks on Israel, which intensified in the years leading up to Operation Protective Edge, are analyzed in detail. The subchapter investigates Hamas' tactics, weaponry, and targets, as well as the impact of these attacks on Israeli civilians and infrastructure. It also evaluates the effectiveness of Hamas' rocket attacks and their long-term implications for the Israeli-Palestinian conflict.

Furthermore, the subchapter addresses the political impact of Operation Protective Edge, both domestically and internationally. It examines the reactions of various political actors, including regional powers and the United Nations, and the subsequent diplomatic efforts to broker a ceasefire. The humanitarian consequences of the Israeli military operation are explored, focusing on the displacement of Palestinians, the destruction of infrastructure, and the loss of civilian lives.

The subchapter also sheds light on the media coverage and propaganda surrounding Operation Protective Edge. It analyzes the role of media outlets and their portrayal of the conflict, as well as the use of social media by both sides as a tool for disseminating information and shaping public opinion.

In addition, the subchapter delves into the legal implications and potential international law violations committed during the military operation. It examines the Israeli Defense Forces' military strategy and tactics, assessing their effectiveness and ethical considerations.

Lastly, the subchapter explores the economic impact of Operation Protective Edge on Gaza, evaluating the long-term consequences for the region's economy and the living conditions of its inhabitants.

Through a comprehensive analysis of these topics, the subchapter provides historians and politicians with valuable insights into the rise of Hamas, the rocket attacks on Israel, and the broader implications of Operation Protective Edge on the Israeli-Palestinian conflict. It aims to foster a deeper understanding of the complexities surrounding this conflict and stimulate informed discussions on the path towards a peaceful resolution.

Triggers for Operation Protective Edge

Operation Protective Edge was a significant Israeli military operation that took place in Gaza in 2014, in response to relentless rocket attacks launched by Hamas. This subchapter aims to delve into the triggers that led to this operation, shedding light on the underlying factors that culminated in such a decisive response.

The escalation of violence began with an increase in the frequency and intensity of rocket attacks by Hamas, which posed a serious threat to the safety and security of Israeli civilians. Over a period of time, these attacks intensified, leaving the Israeli government with no choice but to take action to protect its citizens.

One of the key triggers for Operation Protective Edge was the discovery of a vast network of underground tunnels constructed by Hamas. These intricate tunnels served as conduits for smuggling weapons and militants into Israeli territory, posing an immediate and substantial threat to Israeli citizens. The existence of these tunnels, which were built with the sole purpose of infiltrating Israeli communities, pushed the Israeli Defense Forces (IDF) to initiate the operation.

Moreover, the kidnapping and subsequent murder of three Israeli teenagers by Hamas operatives further fueled the tensions between Israel and Gaza. The Israeli government was left with no option but to respond, as Hamas had demonstrated its brazen disregard for human life and security.

The subchapter will also explore the political impact of Operation Protective Edge, analyzing how it shaped the Israeli government's stance towards Hamas and the Palestinian Authority. It will delve into the humanitarian consequences of the military operation, discussing the impact on civilian populations in Gaza and the challenges faced by humanitarian organizations in providing aid.

Furthermore, the subchapter will shed light on media coverage and propaganda during Operation Protective Edge, highlighting the efforts by both sides to shape public opinion and garner international support. The international reactions to the operation, including diplomatic responses and calls for ceasefires, will also be examined.

In conclusion, this subchapter will provide a comprehensive analysis of the triggers that led to Operation Protective Edge. By examining the various factors that culminated in this military operation, historians and politicians will gain a deeper understanding of the events that unfolded and their implications for the Israeli-Palestinian conflict.

Chapter 2: Political Impact of Operation Protective Edge

Israeli Government's Decision to Launch the Operation

The decision made by the Israeli government to launch Operation Protective Edge in 2014 was a response to the relentless rocket attacks by Hamas, a Palestinian militant group, on Israeli civilian targets. This subchapter explores the factors that influenced the Israeli government's decision and the implications it had on the Israeli-Palestinian conflict.

The Israeli government's primary responsibility is to protect its citizens from any threats to their safety and security. In the years leading up to Operation Protective Edge, Hamas had intensified its rocket attacks, reaching unprecedented levels. These attacks posed a grave danger to the Israeli population, with rockets targeting major cities and towns, including Tel Aviv and Jerusalem. The Israeli government could no longer tolerate this constant threat to its people's lives.

Furthermore, the Israeli government recognized that Hamas was using civilian infrastructure, such as schools and hospitals, as launching pads for its rocket attacks. This deliberate tactic by Hamas put innocent Palestinian civilians at risk and made it difficult for the Israeli Defense Forces (IDF) to respond without causing civilian casualties. The Israeli government had to carefully consider the military strategy that would minimize harm to civilians while effectively neutralizing the threat posed by Hamas.

The decision to launch Operation Protective Edge was not taken lightly. It involved a complex analysis of the military capabilities of Hamas, the potential risks to Israeli civilians, and the long-term implications of a military operation on the Israeli-Palestinian conflict. The Israeli government weighed the options and determined that a decisive response was necessary to restore the security and deter future attacks on its citizens.

This operation had significant political, humanitarian, and legal consequences. It sparked international debates about the proportionality of Israel's response and raised questions about potential violations of international law. The media coverage and propaganda surrounding the operation further complicated the situation, with differing narratives and interpretations of events.

Historians and politicians analyzing Operation Protective Edge must consider the multitude of factors that influenced the Israeli government's decision. The military strategy employed by the IDF, the humanitarian consequences on the civilian population in Gaza, and the long-term implications on the Israeli-Palestinian conflict are all critical aspects to be examined. By studying the decision-making process behind the launch of this operation, we can gain a deeper understanding of the complexities of the Israeli-Palestinian conflict and the challenges faced by policymakers in times of crisis.

International Diplomatic Efforts to End the Conflict

Throughout the course of Operation Protective Edge, various international diplomatic efforts were made in an attempt to bring an end to the conflict between Israel and Hamas. These efforts, initiated by a range of actors including world leaders, international organizations, and regional powers, sought to mediate a ceasefire and facilitate negotiations between the two parties.

One prominent diplomatic initiative was led by the United Nations, with Secretary-General Ban Ki-moon calling for an immediate cessation of hostilities and the restoration of calm. The UN Security Council also held several emergency meetings to discuss the situation and urge both sides to exercise maximum restraint. In addition, the UN established a Commission of Inquiry to investigate allegations of human rights violations and international law violations during the military operation.

The United States, as a key ally of Israel, played an active role in diplomatic efforts. Secretary of State John Kerry traveled to the region multiple times to engage in shuttle diplomacy and broker a ceasefire agreement. Despite significant challenges and setbacks, including the collapse of several proposed truces, Kerry's persistence eventually led to a 72-hour humanitarian ceasefire that allowed for the delivery of aid and the resumption of negotiations.

Regional powers such as Egypt, Qatar, and Turkey also played crucial roles in diplomatic efforts. Egypt, in particular, served as a mediator between Israel and Hamas, proposing ceasefire initiatives and hosting negotiations in Cairo. Qatar and Turkey, on the other hand, had closer ties to Hamas and used their influence to press for the group's demands and advocate for the Palestinian cause on the international stage.

Despite these diplomatic efforts, a lasting ceasefire agreement proved elusive during Operation Protective Edge. The conflict highlighted the underlying complexities and deep-rooted issues of the Israeli-Palestinian conflict, making it difficult to find a sustainable solution. However, the international diplomatic efforts did help mitigate the immediate humanitarian crisis and provide a platform for future negotiations.

In retrospect, the diplomatic efforts during Operation Protective Edge showcased the importance of international engagement and multilateral cooperation in resolving conflicts. The involvement of various actors demonstrated the recognition of the conflict's regional implications and the need for a comprehensive approach. However, the ultimate resolution of the Israeli-Palestinian conflict will require sustained commitment from all parties involved and a genuine desire for peace and reconciliation.

Political Fallout for Israeli and Palestinian Leadership

The 2014 Israeli military operation in Gaza, known as Operation Protective Edge, had significant political ramifications for both Israeli and Palestinian leadership. This subchapter delves into the aftermath and consequences that the operation had on the political landscape of the region.

For Israeli leadership, Operation Protective Edge brought mixed results. On one hand, the operation showcased the Israeli Defense Forces' (IDF) military prowess, successfully neutralizing many Hamas targets and significantly degrading their rocket capabilities. This bolstered the perception of strength and resolve among the Israeli population, increasing support for Prime Minister Benjamin Netanyahu and his government.

However, Operation Protective Edge also exposed the limitations and challenges of Israeli military intervention in Gaza. The operation resulted in a high number of civilian casualties and drew international criticism for the perceived disproportionate use of force. This led to calls for investigations into possible war crimes and violations of international law, putting pressure on Israeli leadership to justify their actions.

For Palestinian leadership, the political fallout of Operation Protective Edge was multi-faceted. On one hand, the operation exposed the vulnerabilities of Hamas and its inability to protect civilians in Gaza. This eroded public trust in Hamas as a governing body, as many Palestinians felt abandoned and left to suffer the consequences of the conflict.

However, Operation Protective Edge also galvanized support for Hamas among certain segments of the Palestinian population, particularly those who viewed armed resistance as the only viable option against Israeli occupation. This polarization deepened existing political divisions between Hamas and the Palestinian Authority (PA), further complicating efforts to achieve unity and a lasting peace agreement with Israel.

The international community's response to Operation Protective Edge played a crucial role in the political fallout for both Israeli and Palestinian leadership. While Israel received support from its traditional allies, particularly the United States, many countries and international organizations condemned the operation's civilian casualties and called for an immediate ceasefire. This put pressure on Israeli leadership to navigate the complex dynamics of international politics and defend their actions.

In conclusion, Operation Protective Edge had profound political consequences for both Israeli and Palestinian leadership. It exposed the strengths and weaknesses of their respective approaches to the conflict, deepening political divisions and raising questions about the long-term viability of their strategies. The fallout from the operation continues to shape the Israeli-Palestinian conflict and will have lasting implications for the region's political landscape.

Chapter 3: Humanitarian Consequences of the Israeli Military Operation

Civilian Casualties in Gaza

One of the most tragic aspects of Operation Protective Edge, the 2014 Israeli military operation in Gaza in response to rocket attacks by Hamas, was the high number of civilian casualties. This subchapter aims to shed light on the devastating impact the conflict had on innocent men, women, and children living in Gaza.

During the operation, the Israeli Defense Forces (IDF) carried out extensive airstrikes and ground operations in an attempt to destroy Hamas' military infrastructure and stop the rocket attacks on Israeli targets. However, the densely populated nature of Gaza, with its limited escape routes and lack of bomb shelters, meant that civilians were caught in the crossfire.

The humanitarian consequences of the Israeli military operation were severe. According to various reports, over 2,000 Palestinians, including many civilians, were killed, and thousands more were injured. The targeting of residential areas, schools, hospitals, and even United Nations facilities raised concerns about the proportionality and legality of the IDF's actions.

Media coverage and propaganda during Operation Protective Edge played a significant role in shaping public perceptions of the conflict. Both sides utilized media platforms to present their narratives and gain international support. This chapter will examine the media's role in disseminating information, the challenges faced by journalists reporting from Gaza, and the use of propaganda by both sides to advance their respective agendas.

The international community reacted with mixed responses to Operation Protective Edge. While some countries supported Israel's right to self-defense, others criticized the disproportionate use of force and the resulting civilian casualties. The legal implications and possible violations of international law during the military operation will be explored, alongside the psychological effects on civilians living in Gaza.

Moreover, this subchapter will analyze the military strategy and tactics employed by the IDF and assess their effectiveness in achieving their objectives. It will also examine the economic impact of Operation Protective Edge on Gaza, as well as the long-term consequences and implications of the conflict on the broader Israeli-Palestinian conflict.

By delving into the civilian casualties in Gaza during Operation Protective Edge, this subchapter will provide valuable insights for historians and politicians. It aims to foster a deeper understanding of the complexities surrounding the conflict, encouraging informed discussions and promoting efforts to prevent similar tragedies in the future.

Displacement and Destruction of Infrastructure

The subchapter "Displacement and Destruction of Infrastructure" delves into one of the most critical aspects of Operation Protective Edge, the 2014 Israeli military operation in Gaza in response to rocket attacks by Hamas. This chapter examines the far-reaching consequences of the conflict on both humanitarian and geopolitical levels. Addressed to historians and politicians, it provides a comprehensive analysis of the impact of the operation, shedding light on its multifaceted dimensions.

Operation Protective Edge resulted in significant displacement and the widespread destruction of vital infrastructure in Gaza. The Israeli Defense Forces (IDF) launched a series of airstrikes and ground incursions, targeting Hamas' military infrastructure but causing collateral damage to civilian areas. As a consequence, numerous homes, schools, hospitals, and essential public facilities were reduced to rubble, leaving thousands of Palestinians homeless and without access to basic services.

This chapter critically evaluates the military strategy and tactics employed by the IDF, focusing on the methods used to target and destroy infrastructure. It examines the legal implications and potential violations of international law during the operation, assessing the IDF's adherence to the principles of proportionality and distinction. The chapter also explores the economic impact of Operation Protective Edge on Gaza, analyzing how the destruction of infrastructure hindered the region's ability to recover and develop.

Moreover, the chapter delves into the psychological effects experienced by civilians living in Gaza during the operation. The constant threat of airstrikes, loss of loved ones, and displacement caused severe trauma among the population, leaving a lasting impact on their mental well-being. By providing an in-depth analysis of these psychological consequences, the chapter aims to raise awareness about the human toll of armed conflicts and the urgent need for psychological support and healing in conflict-affected areas.

Lastly, this subchapter assesses the long-term consequences and implications of Operation Protective Edge on the Israeli-Palestinian conflict. By examining the destruction of infrastructure and its impact on the daily lives of Palestinians, it contributes to a broader understanding of the conflict's underlying dynamics. Furthermore, it highlights the importance of finding a sustainable resolution to the conflict and emphasizes the need to address the root causes of the ongoing violence.

In conclusion, "Displacement and Destruction of Infrastructure" provides a comprehensive analysis of the consequences of Operation Protective Edge. By examining the displacement, destruction of infrastructure, psychological effects, and long-term implications, this chapter aims to shed light on the multifaceted dimensions of the conflict. It serves as a valuable resource for historians and politicians seeking to understand the humanitarian and geopolitical impact of this significant event in the Israeli-Palestinian conflict.

Humanitarian Aid and Relief Efforts

Operation Protective Edge was not only a military operation but also had significant humanitarian consequences for the people living in Gaza. As rockets rained down on Israeli cities and towns, the Israeli Defense Forces (IDF) had to respond, but they also recognized the need to mitigate the impact on civilians caught in the crossfire. This subchapter explores the various humanitarian aid and relief efforts undertaken during the operation.

The IDF implemented several measures to ensure the safety and well-being of civilians in Gaza. These efforts included the establishment of humanitarian corridors to allow the passage of essential goods and aid into Gaza. The IDF also set up field hospitals near the border to provide medical assistance to injured Palestinians.

International aid organizations played a critical role in providing humanitarian relief during Operation Protective Edge. Organizations such as the United Nations Relief and Works Agency for Palestine Refugees in the Near East (UNRWA) and the Red Cross worked tirelessly to deliver food, water, and medical supplies to those in need. These organizations faced immense challenges due to the ongoing conflict, including limited access to affected areas and the risk of indiscriminate attacks.

However, despite these efforts, the humanitarian situation in Gaza deteriorated rapidly. The Israeli blockade, in place since 2007, severely restricted the flow of goods and services into the territory. This, coupled with the destruction of infrastructure during the conflict, created a dire situation for the civilian population.

The media coverage during Operation Protective Edge played a crucial role in shaping international perceptions of the conflict. While the Israeli government emphasized its humanitarian efforts, critics accused Israel of disproportionate use of force and targeting civilian infrastructure. These contrasting narratives influenced the international reactions to the operation and further complicated the delivery of aid and relief efforts.

The long-term consequences of Operation Protective Edge on the Israeli-Palestinian conflict are vast and multifaceted. The humanitarian consequences, including the loss of life, displacement, and destruction of infrastructure, have fueled grievances on both sides. The psychological effects on civilians living in Gaza during the operation cannot be overlooked, as they continue to shape the dynamics of the conflict.

This subchapter delves into the legal implications and international law violations during the military operation. It also analyzes the effectiveness of Hamas rocket attacks on Israeli targets and the economic impact of Operation Protective Edge on Gaza. By examining these aspects, historians and politicians can gain a comprehensive understanding of the complexities surrounding Operation Protective Edge and its long-term implications for the Israeli-Palestinian conflict.

Chapter 4: Media Coverage and Propaganda during Operation Protective Edge

Role of Media in Shaping Public Opinion

The role of media in shaping public opinion has been a subject of great debate and analysis, particularly during times of conflict and crisis. Operation Protective Edge, the 2014 Israeli military operation in Gaza in response to rocket attacks by Hamas, was no exception. In this subchapter, we will explore how the media coverage and propaganda during Operation Protective Edge influenced public opinion, both domestically and internationally.

The media, comprising various outlets such as television, radio, newspapers, and social media platforms, played a crucial role in disseminating information and shaping public perception of the conflict. Historians and politicians can gain valuable insights into the impact of media coverage on public opinion by examining the events of Operation Protective Edge.

During the operation, media coverage was characterized by intense scrutiny, as journalists attempted to cover the conflict from different perspectives. However, it is important to acknowledge that media outlets often have their own biases and agendas, which can influence the way information is presented to the public. This bias was evident during Operation Protective Edge, with both Israeli and Palestinian media accused of engaging in propaganda to further their respective narratives.

The media's portrayal of the conflict had significant political implications. Politicians, aware of the power of media in shaping public opinion, sought to control the narrative by carefully managing their interactions with journalists. This strategic manipulation of the media helped politicians shape public opinion in favor of their objectives, whether it was garnering support for the military operation or criticizing Israel's actions.

Furthermore, the media coverage had a profound impact on the psychological well-being of civilians living in Gaza during the operation. The constant bombardment of images and stories of destruction and suffering fueled fear and anxiety among the population. This psychological trauma had long-lasting effects on the mental health of individuals, particularly children, who were exposed to the horrors of war through media coverage.

Moreover, media coverage of Operation Protective Edge had legal implications, particularly regarding potential violations of international law. The media played a crucial role in documenting and disseminating evidence of alleged war crimes committed by both sides. This coverage prompted international organizations and legal experts to investigate and hold accountable those responsible for potential violations.

In conclusion, the media's role in shaping public opinion during Operation Protective Edge cannot be underestimated. Historians and politicians studying the conflict must critically analyze the media coverage and propaganda to gain a comprehensive understanding of the impact on public perception, political implications, psychological effects on civilians, legal implications, and long-term consequences for the Israeli-Palestinian conflict.

Analysis of Media Bias and Propaganda Techniques Used

In the age of information, the role of media in shaping public opinion and influencing political outcomes cannot be understated. In the case of Operation Protective Edge, the 2014 Israeli military operation in Gaza in response to rocket attacks by Hamas, media bias and propaganda techniques played a significant role in shaping the narrative surrounding the conflict. This subchapter aims to dissect the various strategies employed by both sides to manipulate public perception and analyze their implications.

Media coverage during Operation Protective Edge was marred by allegations of bias from both Israeli and Palestinian perspectives. Historians and politicians must critically analyze the media's portrayal of the conflict to understand the larger political and historical implications. Reports of civilian casualties, destruction of infrastructure, and displacement of Palestinians dominated the headlines, often painting Israel as an aggressor and Hamas as a victim. On the other hand, Israeli media highlighted the threat posed by Hamas rockets and the military's efforts to protect its citizens.

Propaganda techniques were also employed by both sides to shape public opinion. Hamas utilized imagery and narratives that portrayed Palestinians as victims of Israeli aggression, evoking sympathy and garnering support from international audiences. The Israeli Defense Forces, on the other hand, employed media manipulation to emphasize their efforts to minimize civilian casualties and justify their military response.

Understanding the media bias and propaganda techniques used during Operation Protective Edge is crucial for historians and politicians. It allows them to critically assess the information presented to the public and draw objective conclusions. By dissecting the narratives and analyzing the motives behind media coverage, we can gain a deeper understanding of the conflict's political impact, humanitarian consequences, and long-term implications on the Israeli-Palestinian conflict.

Moreover, the subchapter will explore the international reactions to media coverage during Operation Protective Edge. It will delve into how different countries and organizations responded to the conflict and whether their responses were influenced by media bias. Additionally, the psychological effects on civilians living in Gaza during the operation, such as trauma and fear, will be examined, shedding light on the human cost of media manipulation.

Furthermore, the subchapter will assess the legal implications and potential international law violations committed by both sides during the conflict. It will analyze the military tactics employed by the Israeli Defense Forces and determine whether they adhered to international humanitarian law. Additionally, the economic impact of Operation Protective Edge on Gaza will be examined, highlighting the long-lasting consequences of the conflict on the region's economy.

In conclusion, media bias and propaganda techniques played a pivotal role in shaping public perception during Operation Protective Edge. Historians and politicians must critically analyze the media coverage to obtain a comprehensive understanding of the conflict's political impact, humanitarian consequences, and long-term implications. By dissecting the narratives and examining the motives behind media bias, we can unravel the truth and contribute to a more nuanced understanding of the Israeli-Palestinian conflict.

Impact of Media Coverage on International Perception

Media coverage plays a pivotal role in shaping international perception during times of conflict. This subchapter examines the impact of media coverage on international perception during Operation Protective Edge, the 2014 Israeli military operation in Gaza in response to rocket attacks by Hamas. Addressed to historians and politicians, this section provides a comprehensive analysis of the various aspects related to media coverage during the operation.

The media has the power to influence public opinion and shape international responses to conflicts. During Operation Protective Edge, media coverage and propaganda played a significant role in shaping how the world perceived the Israeli military response. This subchapter delves into the strategies employed by both sides to portray their narrative and influence public opinion. It explores the use of social media, mainstream news outlets, and propaganda campaigns to shape international perception.

Furthermore, this subchapter analyzes the international reactions to Operation Protective Edge, taking into consideration the role media coverage played in shaping these responses. It examines the varying levels of support, condemnation, and calls for intervention from world leaders, governments, and international organizations. By examining the impact of media coverage on international perception, historians and politicians can gain insights into the effectiveness of different strategies employed by the conflicting parties.

Moreover, this subchapter explores the psychological effects on civilians living in Gaza during the operation. It delves into the trauma and fear experienced by the population, exacerbated by media coverage and the constant exposure to graphic images and reports. By understanding the psychological effects on civilians, policymakers can develop more effective strategies for conflict resolution and humanitarian aid.

In addition, this subchapter delves into the legal implications and international law violations during the military operation. It critically analyzes the actions of both parties and examines how media coverage influenced the perception of these violations. By understanding the legal implications and violations, policymakers and historians can assess the accountability of the conflicting parties and work towards preventing future violations.

Overall, this subchapter offers historians and politicians a comprehensive analysis of the impact of media coverage on international perception during Operation Protective Edge. By understanding the role of media in shaping public opinion, policymakers can make more informed decisions and work towards conflict resolution and peacebuilding.

Chapter 5: International Reactions to Operation Protective Edge

Responses from Arab and Muslim Countries

The 2014 Israeli military operation in Gaza, known as Operation Protective Edge, sparked a range of responses from Arab and Muslim countries across the world. This subchapter explores the various reactions from these nations and their implications on the Israeli-Palestinian conflict.

Arab and Muslim countries, while united in their support for the Palestinian cause, displayed a diversity of responses to Operation Protective Edge. Some nations condemned Israel's actions outright, accusing it of disproportionate use of force and violation of international law. These countries, including Egypt, Jordan, and Turkey, called for an immediate ceasefire and demanded that Israel be held accountable for its actions.

However, other countries in the region took a more nuanced approach. Saudi Arabia, for instance, initially criticized Hamas for escalating the conflict and urged both sides to exercise restraint. This response highlights the complex dynamics at play within the Arab world, where countries balance their support for the Palestinian cause with their own strategic interests.

Moreover, the responses from Arab and Muslim countries were not limited to official statements alone. Public demonstrations and protests erupted in many nations, expressing solidarity with the people of Gaza. These demonstrations often resulted in clashes with local security forces, underscoring the deep-rooted emotions surrounding the Israeli-Palestinian conflict.

The responses from Arab and Muslim countries also had political implications within their own borders. Governments faced pressure from their populations to take a stronger stance against Israel, leading some to sever diplomatic ties or impose economic sanctions. This further strained regional relations and highlighted the divide between those who supported Israel's right to defend itself and those who condemned its actions.

Historians and politicians must analyze these responses to gain a comprehensive understanding of the broader context of Operation Protective Edge. By examining the various positions taken by Arab and Muslim countries, scholars can better comprehend the regional dynamics and the impact of the conflict on the Israeli-Palestinian relationship. This analysis can inform future diplomatic efforts and facilitate a more nuanced approach to resolving the long-standing conflict.

In conclusion, the responses from Arab and Muslim countries during Operation Protective Edge were varied, ranging from condemnations to calls for restraint. These reactions had political, social, and economic consequences, both within the nations themselves and in the broader context of the Israeli-Palestinian conflict. Understanding these responses is crucial for historians and politicians seeking to grasp the complexities of the conflict and work towards a peaceful resolution.

Role of the United Nations and International Organizations

The role played by the United Nations (UN) and other international organizations during Operation Protective Edge in 2014 was of utmost importance. Historians and politicians have extensively studied and analyzed the actions and impact of these entities, recognizing their significant contributions to addressing the complexities of the conflict and its aftermath.

The UN, as the primary international forum for promoting peace and security, played a crucial role in mediating between the conflicting parties and facilitating negotiations for a ceasefire. Through the efforts of Secretary-General Ban Ki-moon and his envoys, the UN worked tirelessly to bring about a cessation of hostilities and prevent further loss of life.

International organizations, such as the International Committee of the Red Cross (ICRC) and various humanitarian agencies, also played a vital role in providing essential aid and assistance to the affected population. These organizations worked tirelessly to deliver medical supplies, food, and shelter to civilians affected by the conflict, mitigating the humanitarian consequences of the Israeli military operation.

Additionally, the UN and other international organizations were instrumental in documenting and investigating alleged human rights violations and international law violations during Operation Protective Edge. This documentation not only aimed to hold accountable those responsible for these violations but also served as a crucial tool for the legal implications of the military operation.

Furthermore, the UN and international organizations assisted in assessing the economic impact of Operation Protective Edge on Gaza. These assessments helped policymakers understand the long-term consequences of the conflict on the already fragile economy of the region, highlighting the urgent need for reconstruction and development initiatives.

The international reactions to Operation Protective Edge were diverse, with different countries and regional blocs expressing varying degrees of support or condemnation for the Israeli military response. The UN and international organizations played a key role in harmonizing these reactions and facilitating diplomatic efforts to find a sustainable resolution to the Israeli-Palestinian conflict.

In conclusion, the role of the United Nations and international organizations during Operation Protective Edge cannot be overstated. Historians and politicians continue to study and analyze their actions, recognizing the significant impact they had on addressing the political, humanitarian, legal, and economic dimensions of the conflict. Their efforts in mediating, providing aid, documenting violations, and facilitating international reactions were crucial in shaping the long-term consequences and implications of Operation Protective Edge on the Israeli-Palestinian conflict.

Support and Criticism from Western Nations

Operation Protective Edge, the 2014 Israeli military operation in Gaza in response to rocket attacks by Hamas, garnered significant attention and elicited a range of responses from Western nations. Historians and politicians have analyzed the support and criticism expressed by these countries, which have had both immediate and long-term implications for the Israeli-Palestinian conflict.

Several Western nations, particularly the United States, offered unwavering support for Israel during Operation Protective Edge. They emphasized Israel's right to defend itself against rocket attacks and condemned Hamas for using civilian infrastructure as launching sites. The U.S. government, in particular, acknowledged Israel's efforts to minimize civilian casualties and reaffirmed its commitment to Israel's security. Historians and politicians have argued that this support bolstered Israel's morale and justified its military actions.

However, not all Western nations shared the same perspective. Some European countries, such as France and the United Kingdom, expressed concerns about the proportionality of Israel's response and the high number of civilian casualties in Gaza. They called for an immediate ceasefire and urged Israel to exercise restraint. Critics argued that Israel's military tactics, including the targeting of residential areas and infrastructure, violated international law and exacerbated the humanitarian crisis in Gaza.

The divergent reactions from Western nations during Operation Protective Edge also highlighted the complexities of the Israeli-Palestinian conflict and exposed underlying political dynamics. Historians and politicians have examined how Western countries' responses were influenced by domestic political considerations, historical ties, and regional alliances. This scrutiny has shed light on the challenges of achieving a balanced and impartial approach to the conflict.

Furthermore, the support and criticism from Western nations had significant implications for the long-term prospects of peace in the region. The international community's response shaped public opinion, influenced negotiations, and impacted the perception of Israel's legitimacy. Historians and politicians have analyzed how these reactions have affected the overall dynamics of the conflict, including the prospects for future peace agreements and the role of international actors in resolving the Israeli-Palestinian dispute.

In conclusion, the support and criticism from Western nations during Operation Protective Edge had a profound impact on various aspects of the Israeli-Palestinian conflict. Historians and politicians continue to analyze these reactions, seeking to understand their immediate consequences and long-term implications. By examining the international response, it becomes evident that the conflict is not only a local issue but one that resonates with global audiences and carries significant geopolitical implications.

Chapter 6: Psychological Effects on Civilians Living in Gaza during the Operation

Trauma and Mental Health Issues

The subchapter "Trauma and Mental Health Issues" explores the profound psychological effects experienced by civilians living in Gaza during Operation Protective Edge, the 2014 Israeli military operation in response to rocket attacks by Hamas. This section delves into the long-lasting consequences and implications of the operation on the Israeli-Palestinian conflict, shedding light on the humanitarian and psychological toll it took on the people involved.

Operation Protective Edge not only resulted in significant physical destruction but also left behind deep emotional scars on both sides. This subchapter examines the psychological impact of the conflict on civilians, particularly those living in Gaza. It delves into the trauma experienced by individuals who endured constant fear, loss, and displacement during the operation. By analyzing firsthand accounts and scholarly research, this section provides a comprehensive understanding of the mental health issues that arose in the aftermath of the conflict.

The chapter begins by discussing the immediate psychological effects of the operation, including post-traumatic stress disorder (PTSD), anxiety, and depression, which affected a significant portion of the population in Gaza. It explores the challenges faced by mental health professionals in providing adequate support and treatment to those in need, given the limited resources and infrastructure in the region.

Furthermore, this subchapter delves into the long-term consequences of trauma and mental health issues on the Israeli-Palestinian conflict. It addresses how untreated psychological trauma can perpetuate cycles of violence and hinder the possibility of reconciliation and peace. By examining the psychological impact on individuals, families, and communities, historians and politicians gain valuable insight into the complex dynamics that perpetuate the conflict.

Additionally, this section explores the legal implications and violations of international law during Operation Protective Edge, particularly regarding the treatment of civilians and the responsibility of the Israeli Defense Forces. By highlighting the connection between mental health issues and human rights violations, this subchapter sheds light on the broader consequences of the conflict on a global scale.

In conclusion, this subchapter provides a comprehensive analysis of the trauma and mental health issues that emerged during Operation Protective Edge. By understanding the psychological toll of the conflict, historians and politicians can gain a deeper appreciation for the complexity of the Israeli-Palestinian conflict, the consequences of military operations, and the urgent need for mental health support and intervention in post-conflict settings.

Impact on Children and Families

The 2014 Israeli military operation in Gaza, known as Operation Protective Edge, had far-reaching consequences for the children and families living in the conflict zone. This subchapter aims to shed light on the often overlooked humanitarian aspect of the operation, focusing on the direct impact on the most vulnerable members of society.

During the operation, countless children and families in Gaza experienced unimaginable suffering. The indiscriminate bombing campaigns and ground incursions by the Israeli Defense Forces (IDF) resulted in the deaths of hundreds of Palestinian children and the displacement of thousands more. The destruction of homes, schools, and hospitals further exacerbated the already dire living conditions in Gaza, leaving families without adequate shelter, access to clean water, and medical care.

The psychological effects on children living in Gaza during the operation were profound. Constant exposure to violence and fear caused significant trauma, resulting in long-term emotional and psychological damage. Children witnessed the loss of loved ones, experienced displacement, and lived in constant fear for their lives. These experiences will likely have lasting effects on their mental well-being and future prospects.

The international community's response to the humanitarian crisis in Gaza was mixed. While some countries and organizations provided aid and called for an immediate ceasefire, others remained silent or offered only token gestures. The lack of a unified and decisive international response further exacerbated the suffering of children and families in Gaza.

Moreover, the military tactics employed by the IDF during the operation raised significant concerns about potential violations of international law. The targeting of civilian infrastructure and the use of disproportionate force in densely populated areas drew criticism from human rights organizations and sparked debates about the legality of the operation.

The long-term consequences of Operation Protective Edge on the Israeli-Palestinian conflict cannot be understated. The destruction and suffering experienced by children and families in Gaza only serve to deepen the grievances and animosity between the two sides. The operation further entrenched the cycle of violence, making a peaceful resolution to the conflict even more elusive.

In conclusion, Operation Protective Edge had a devastating impact on children and families in Gaza. The humanitarian consequences of the Israeli military operation, coupled with the psychological effects on civilians, highlight the urgent need for a comprehensive and lasting resolution to the Israeli-Palestinian conflict. It is imperative for historians and politicians to examine these consequences in order to inform future strategies and policies that promote peace, justice, and security for all parties involved.

Post-Traumatic Stress Disorder and Coping Mechanisms

In the wake of Operation Protective Edge, the 2014 Israeli military operation in Gaza, the psychological effects on civilians living in the conflict-ridden region cannot be overlooked. The chapter titled "Post-Traumatic Stress Disorder and Coping Mechanisms" delves into the profound impact of this military operation on the mental health of the individuals caught in the crossfire, shedding light on the coping mechanisms they employed to navigate their traumatic experiences.

The chapter begins by outlining the nature of Post-Traumatic Stress Disorder (PTSD) and its prevalence among the civilian population in Gaza following Operation Protective Edge. Through interviews, case studies, and expert analysis, the authors provide a comprehensive understanding of the psychological trauma endured by individuals who witnessed or experienced the violence firsthand.

Examining the coping mechanisms adopted by the affected population, the chapter highlights the resilience and resourcefulness demonstrated by these individuals in the face of adversity. From seeking social support to engaging in religious practices, various strategies are explored to showcase the diverse range of coping mechanisms employed.

Furthermore, the chapter delves into the role of community-based organizations and mental health professionals in providing support and assistance to those suffering from PTSD. It analyzes the effectiveness of these interventions in mitigating the long-term psychological consequences of the military operation.

Addressing an audience of historians and politicians, this chapter serves as a critical resource for understanding the human cost of Operation Protective Edge. By shedding light on the psychological toll inflicted on the civilian population, it emphasizes the importance of considering the long-term consequences and implications of such military operations on the Israeli-Palestinian conflict.

Moreover, the chapter situates the discussion within the broader context of the conflict, examining how PTSD and coping mechanisms intersect with the political, humanitarian, and legal dimensions of Operation Protective Edge. By providing a multidimensional analysis, it offers valuable insights into the complex dynamics at play in the aftermath of this military operation.

In conclusion, "Post-Traumatic Stress Disorder and Coping Mechanisms" offers a comprehensive exploration of the psychological effects on civilians living in Gaza during Operation Protective Edge. By examining coping mechanisms and the role of support networks, it provides a nuanced understanding of the challenges faced by individuals in the aftermath of conflict. This chapter serves as a crucial resource for historians and politicians seeking to comprehend the multifaceted implications of this military operation on both individual and collective levels.

Chapter 7: Legal Implications and International Law Violations during the Military Operation

Analysis of Israeli and Hamas Compliance with International Law

One of the key aspects to be examined in the aftermath of Operation Protective Edge is the compliance of both Israeli and Hamas forces with international law. This analysis is crucial for historians and politicians seeking to understand the legal implications and violations during the military operation.

Israeli Defense Forces (IDF) have long claimed to adhere to international law while conducting military operations. However, critics argue that the IDF's actions during Operation Protective Edge raise serious concerns about their compliance with international humanitarian law. The extensive use of artillery and airstrikes in densely populated areas of Gaza resulted in a high number of civilian casualties, leading to accusations of indiscriminate attacks and disproportionate use of force.

On the other hand, Hamas, as a non-state actor, is also bound by international law. However, the group has been accused of numerous violations during the conflict. Hamas's tactics of using civilian areas, including hospitals and schools, for military purposes such as storing weapons and launching attacks, have raised questions about their compliance with the principle of distinction between combatants and civilians.

To fully understand the extent of the violations committed by both sides, it is essential to examine specific cases that exemplify the breaches of international law. Instances such as the shelling of UN schools and hospitals by the IDF and the launching of rockets from residential areas by Hamas need to be analyzed in detail.

Moreover, this analysis should also consider the actions taken by the international community to hold both parties accountable for their violations. The role of international organizations such as the United Nations and the International Criminal Court in investigating and prosecuting potential war crimes should be explored.

By critically evaluating the compliance of Israeli and Hamas forces with international law, historians and politicians can gain valuable insights into the legal implications and violations during Operation Protective Edge. This analysis will contribute to a comprehensive understanding of the conflict and its long-term consequences on the Israeli-Palestinian conflict, as well as inform future discussions on conflict resolution and the protection of civilians in armed conflicts.

Investigations and Legal Challenges

The subchapter "Investigations and Legal Challenges" delves into the extensive investigations and legal implications that unfolded in the aftermath of Operation Protective Edge. This section explores the various inquiries and legal challenges faced by the Israeli military and the international community.

In the wake of the 2014 Israeli military operation in Gaza, multiple investigations were launched to examine the conduct of both the Israeli Defense Forces (IDF) and Hamas. These investigations sought to determine whether any violations of international law had occurred during the conflict.

For the IDF, internal investigations were conducted to evaluate allegations of misconduct and potential war crimes. These investigations analyzed the actions of individual soldiers, commanders, and decision-makers to ensure adherence to international humanitarian law and the rules of engagement.

Simultaneously, international organizations, such as the United Nations Human Rights Council (UNHRC), initiated their own investigations into the conduct of both parties involved. These investigations aimed to assess whether violations of international law had taken place, including the disproportionate use of force, targeting of civilians, and destruction of infrastructure.

The legal challenges stemming from Operation Protective Edge extended beyond investigations. Numerous legal cases were brought before international courts, such as the International Criminal Court (ICC), accusing both the Israeli military and Hamas of war crimes and human rights abuses.

Furthermore, the legal implications of the conflict raised questions regarding the applicability of international law in asymmetric warfare and the challenges of holding non-state actors accountable for their actions.

This subchapter also explores the controversies surrounding the legal frameworks employed by both sides to justify their actions. It examines the legal interpretations of self-defense, proportionality, and distinction between combatants and civilians, which played a crucial role in shaping the narrative of the conflict.

The investigations and legal challenges discussed in this subchapter shed light on the complexities of holding parties accountable for their actions in a conflict marked by asymmetry and blurred lines between combatants and non-combatants. These investigations and legal proceedings have far-reaching implications for future conflicts and the Israeli-Palestinian conflict as a whole.

By examining the investigations and legal challenges surrounding Operation Protective Edge, historians and politicians gain valuable insights into the complexities of modern warfare, the role of international law, and the potential for accountability in conflicts where civilian populations are heavily affected.

Implications for International Humanitarian Law

The 2014 Israeli military operation in Gaza, known as Operation Protective Edge, had profound implications for international humanitarian law (IHL). This subchapter explores the legal framework within which the operation took place and the violations that were alleged to have occurred.

International humanitarian law, also known as the laws of war, is a body of rules and principles that seek to minimize the suffering caused by armed conflicts and protect those who are not or no longer participating in the hostilities. It is based on principles of humanity, distinction, proportionality, and necessity.

During Operation Protective Edge, allegations of violations of IHL were raised by various human rights organizations and international bodies. These included accusations of indiscriminate attacks on civilians, targeting of civilian infrastructure, and the disproportionate use of force.

One of the key legal issues was the distinction between combatants and civilians. Under IHL, civilians are protected from direct attack unless and for such time as they directly participate in hostilities. The Israeli Defense Forces (IDF) were accused of failing to adequately distinguish between legitimate military targets and civilians, leading to a high number of civilian casualties.

Another controversial aspect was the targeting of civilian infrastructure, such as schools, hospitals, and water facilities. IHL prohibits attacks on civilian objects unless they are being used for military purposes. The IDF was criticized for alleged attacks on civilian infrastructure without sufficient justification.

Proportionality and necessity were also central to the legal debate surrounding Operation Protective Edge. These principles require that the use of force be proportionate to the military advantage anticipated and that military objectives can only be pursued if they are of military necessity. Critics argued that the IDF's response was disproportionate and went beyond what was necessary to achieve its military objectives.

The legal implications of Operation Protective Edge go beyond the specific incident and have broader ramifications for the Israeli-Palestinian conflict. The operation highlighted the challenges of applying IHL in asymmetric conflicts, where one party has a technologically superior military and the other relies on guerrilla tactics. It also raised questions about the effectiveness of the international legal framework in holding parties accountable for violations.

In conclusion, Operation Protective Edge raised significant questions about the adherence to and enforcement of international humanitarian law. The alleged violations during the operation underscore the need for further examination and accountability to ensure that the principles of IHL are respected in future conflicts.

Chapter 8: Military Strategy and Tactics Employed by the Israeli Defense Forces

Objectives and Operational Planning

In this subchapter, we delve into the objectives and operational planning behind Operation Protective Edge, the 2014 Israeli Military Operation in Gaza in response to rocket attacks by Hamas. This section is tailored to historians and politicians interested in understanding the intricacies of this significant event in the Israeli-Palestinian conflict.

The objectives of Operation Protective Edge were multi-faceted and aimed at restoring peace and security to Israeli citizens while significantly weakening Hamas' rocket capabilities. Through meticulous operational planning, the Israeli Defense Forces (IDF) sought to protect Israeli civilians, dismantle Hamas' underground tunnel network, and degrade their ability to launch rockets into Israeli territory.

Operational planning involved a combination of intelligence gathering, military strategy, and tactical execution. The IDF meticulously studied Hamas' infrastructure, identified rocket launching sites, and devised plans to neutralize these threats. The use of advanced technology, such as aerial surveillance and precision airstrikes, allowed for surgical strikes on key Hamas targets while minimizing collateral damage.

The political impact of Operation Protective Edge cannot be understated. It was a decisive move by the Israeli government to protect its citizens and assert its authority in the face of ongoing rocket attacks. The military operation had far-reaching consequences, including shaping public opinion, influencing international politics, and impacting the Israeli-Palestinian conflict.

The humanitarian consequences of the Israeli military operation were significant, with a large number of civilian casualties and widespread destruction of infrastructure in Gaza. This subchapter will explore the human toll of the operation, including the displacement of thousands of Palestinians and the challenges faced by humanitarian organizations in providing assistance.

Media coverage and propaganda during Operation Protective Edge played a crucial role in shaping public opinion both locally and internationally. This section will examine the different narratives presented by Israeli and Palestinian media outlets, the use of social media as a tool for propaganda, and the challenges faced by journalists in reporting from conflict zones.

Furthermore, international reactions to Operation Protective Edge varied greatly, with some countries condemning Israel's actions while others offered support. We will analyze the diplomatic fallout from the operation and its implications for future peace negotiations.

Lastly, this subchapter will explore the long-term consequences and implications of Operation Protective Edge on the Israeli-Palestinian conflict. It will assess whether the military operation achieved its objectives, the impact on the peace process, and the potential for renewed hostilities.

In conclusion, this subchapter provides a comprehensive analysis of the objectives and operational planning behind Operation Protective Edge. It examines the political, humanitarian, and strategic aspects of the military operation, offering historians and politicians valuable insights into this pivotal event and its long-term implications.

Air and Ground Operations

The air and ground operations during Operation Protective Edge played a crucial role in shaping the outcome of the 2014 Israeli military operation in Gaza. This subchapter aims to provide a comprehensive analysis of the strategies, tactics, and implications of these operations, shedding light on their historical significance and political impact.

The Israeli Defense Forces (IDF) adopted a multifaceted approach that combined air strikes and ground incursions to counter the rocket attacks launched by Hamas. The IDF utilized its air superiority to conduct precision strikes on Hamas infrastructure, targeting rocket launchers, tunnels, weapons depots, and command centers. These airstrikes were meticulously planned to minimize civilian casualties, with the IDF employing advanced intelligence gathering and targeting technologies. However, the densely populated nature of Gaza posed a significant challenge, and despite the IDF's efforts, collateral damage and civilian casualties were inevitable.

In addition to air strikes, the IDF executed ground incursions into Gaza to neutralize Hamas operatives and dismantle their infrastructure. These operations involved a combination of infantry, armored units, and special forces, aiming to disrupt Hamas' command and control capabilities while minimizing Israeli casualties. The ground operations were characterized by meticulous planning, intelligence gathering, and coordination with air support, enabling the IDF to identify and destroy Hamas' underground tunnel network, which served as a major conduit for smuggling weapons and launching attacks on Israeli soil.

The military strategy and tactics employed by the IDF were subject to intense scrutiny both during and after the operation. Critics raised concerns about potential violations of international law, particularly regarding the proportionality of force used and the impact on civilian populations. The legal implications of the military operation and its compliance with international law will be explored in detail in subsequent chapters.

Operation Protective Edge had far-reaching consequences beyond the immediate military objectives. The economic impact on Gaza was significant, with infrastructure damage and disruption to essential services exacerbating an already dire humanitarian situation. The psychological effects on civilians living in Gaza during the operation were profound, as they endured constant fear, trauma, and loss. The media coverage and propaganda surrounding the operation, as well as the international reactions to it, further shaped public opinion and influenced political discourse.

This subchapter aims to provide a comprehensive analysis of the air and ground operations during Operation Protective Edge, exploring their historical significance, political impact, and implications for the Israeli-Palestinian conflict. By examining the military strategies employed, their compliance with international law, and their humanitarian consequences, this subchapter seeks to provide a balanced and nuanced perspective for historians and politicians studying this critical period in the Israeli-Palestinian conflict.

Use of Technology and Intelligence

One of the key factors that played a significant role in the success of Operation Protective Edge, the 2014 Israeli military operation in Gaza in response to rocket attacks by Hamas, was the effective use of technology and intelligence. This subchapter aims to shed light on the crucial role that technology and intelligence played during this operation.

The Israeli Defense Forces (IDF) heavily relied on advanced technological systems to gather intelligence and carry out targeted operations against Hamas militants. These systems included surveillance drones, satellite imagery, and cyber intelligence capabilities, which provided real-time information on Hamas's movements, rocket launch sites, and underground tunnels. By utilizing these technologies, the IDF was able to accurately locate and neutralize Hamas operatives, minimizing collateral damage and civilian casualties.

Moreover, the IDF employed cutting-edge communication systems that greatly enhanced the coordination and effectiveness of their operations. Through secure and encrypted communication channels, commanders could relay information, coordinate troop movements, and share real-time intelligence, ensuring a synchronized and efficient response to Hamas's rocket attacks.

The use of technology also extended to the defense systems deployed by Israel to intercept and neutralize Hamas rockets. The Iron Dome, a state-of-the-art missile defense system, played a crucial role in intercepting and destroying incoming rockets, protecting Israeli civilians and infrastructure. Its advanced radar and tracking systems accurately identified and engaged threats, effectively minimizing the impact of Hamas rocket attacks.

Furthermore, the IDF utilized advanced cyber warfare techniques to disrupt Hamas's communication networks and disable their cyber infrastructure. This not only hindered Hamas's ability to launch coordinated attacks but also allowed the IDF to gain valuable intelligence on Hamas's capabilities and intentions.

In conclusion, the effective use of technology and intelligence was instrumental in the success of Operation Protective Edge. The IDF's ability to gather real-time intelligence, coordinate operations, and neutralize Hamas's rocket launch sites greatly contributed to minimizing civilian casualties and protecting Israeli civilians. Furthermore, the advanced defense systems, such as the Iron Dome, played a vital role in intercepting and neutralizing Hamas rockets, ensuring the safety of Israeli cities. The use of cyber warfare techniques also disrupted Hamas's communication networks and hindered their ability to launch coordinated attacks. The intelligent and strategic use of technology undoubtedly played a significant role in the outcome of Operation Protective Edge.

Chapter 9: Economic Impact of Operation Protective Edge on Gaza

Destruction of Gaza's Economy and Infrastructure

The destruction of Gaza's economy and infrastructure during Operation Protective Edge in 2014 was a devastating consequence of the Israeli military operation in response to rocket attacks by Hamas. This subchapter aims to provide a comprehensive analysis of the economic impact that this operation had on Gaza, shedding light on the long-term consequences it had on the Israeli-Palestinian conflict.

Operation Protective Edge resulted in widespread destruction of Gaza's infrastructure, including residential buildings, schools, hospitals, and vital utilities such as water and electricity. The Israeli Defense Forces justified these actions as necessary to target Hamas militants and their rocket launching sites. However, the scale of destruction raised concerns among historians and politicians about the proportionality of the response and the impact it had on civilians.

The economic repercussions were severe. Gaza's already fragile economy, heavily reliant on international aid and exports, was brought to its knees. Industries such as agriculture and manufacturing were severely disrupted, leaving thousands unemployed and exacerbating poverty levels. The blockade imposed by Israel on Gaza further compounded the economic crisis by limiting the flow of goods and stifling trade opportunities.

The destruction of infrastructure also hindered the delivery of humanitarian aid and reconstruction efforts. The already strained resources of international organizations and NGOs were stretched to their limits, making the task of rebuilding Gaza's shattered economy and infrastructure a daunting challenge.

Furthermore, the economic impact of Operation Protective Edge had broader political implications. The devastation caused by the Israeli military operation fueled anti-Israel sentiment and strengthened support for Hamas among Palestinians. This polarization further complicated the prospects for peace negotiations and the resolution of the Israeli-Palestinian conflict.

To fully understand the economic impact, it is crucial to analyze the international reactions to Operation Protective Edge. The response from the international community varied, with some countries condemning the Israeli military operation as excessive and others expressing support for Israel's right to defend itself. These reactions influenced the flow of aid and assistance to Gaza, further shaping the economic recovery process.

This subchapter will also explore the legal implications and international law violations during the military operation. Many experts argue that the extensive destruction of civilian infrastructure may have constituted violations of international humanitarian law and the principles of proportionality and distinction.

In conclusion, the destruction of Gaza's economy and infrastructure during Operation Protective Edge had far-reaching consequences for both Palestinians and Israelis. The economic impact continues to be felt, further exacerbating the already complex Israeli-Palestinian conflict. Understanding the economic dimension of this military operation is essential for historians and politicians seeking to find sustainable solutions and pave the way for a peaceful resolution.

Impact on Trade and Employment

The 2014 Israeli military operation in Gaza, known as Operation Protective Edge, had significant implications for trade and employment in the region. The conflict, triggered by rocket attacks launched by Hamas, resulted in a devastating blow to the economy of Gaza and had long-lasting effects on the livelihoods of its residents.

One of the immediate impacts of Operation Protective Edge was the disruption of trade and commerce in Gaza. The Israeli blockade, which had been in place since 2007, was tightened during the operation, severely limiting the flow of goods and services in and out of the region. This had a detrimental effect on local businesses, many of which relied on imports and exports for their survival. The closure of border crossings and restrictions on the movement of goods not only stifled economic growth but also led to shortages of essential supplies, including food, medicine, and fuel.

Furthermore, the destruction of infrastructure, such as factories, farms, and agricultural lands, further hampered economic activity in Gaza. The Israeli airstrikes and ground offensive targeted not only military installations but also civilian infrastructure, causing extensive damage to businesses and industries. The loss of infrastructure and assets resulted in the loss of jobs and income for many Gazans, exacerbating the already high levels of unemployment and poverty in the region.

The impact on employment was not limited to Gaza alone. Israel, too, experienced economic consequences as a result of the conflict. The constant threat of rocket attacks forced many businesses in southern Israel to shut down temporarily, causing significant disruptions in trade and employment. The psychological toll on workers, who lived in constant fear of rocket attacks, also affected productivity and economic output.

In the long term, the economic impact of Operation Protective Edge on Gaza and Israel had profound implications for the Israeli-Palestinian conflict. The worsening economic conditions in Gaza, coupled with high levels of unemployment and poverty, served as a breeding ground for resentment and desperation. This, in turn, fueled further violence and extremism, making a peaceful resolution to the conflict even more challenging.

In conclusion, Operation Protective Edge had a significant impact on trade and employment in Gaza and Israel. The blockade, destruction of infrastructure, and disruptions in business activities caused immense economic hardships for both sides. The long-term consequences of this economic devastation on the Israeli-Palestinian conflict cannot be overlooked, as it further deepened the divide and hindered efforts for peace and stability in the region.

International Aid and Reconstruction Efforts

During Operation Protective Edge, the 2014 Israeli military operation in Gaza in response to rocket attacks by Hamas, international aid and reconstruction efforts played a crucial role in alleviating the humanitarian crisis and rebuilding the war-torn region. This subchapter examines the various aspects of international aid and reconstruction efforts, shedding light on their significance and impact.

The humanitarian consequences of the Israeli military operation were devastating, with a significant loss of civilian lives and widespread destruction of infrastructure. In response, numerous countries and international organizations stepped forward to provide assistance to the affected population. Humanitarian aid in the form of food, medicine, and shelter was urgently needed to address the immediate needs of the displaced and injured.

Furthermore, reconstruction efforts aimed at rebuilding Gaza's infrastructure, including homes, schools, hospitals, and water and sanitation facilities, were initiated by the international community. These efforts were vital in restoring normalcy and providing a sense of hope for the people of Gaza, who had endured immense suffering during the conflict.

The media coverage and propaganda surrounding Operation Protective Edge played a crucial role in highlighting the need for international aid and reconstruction efforts. The global community witnessed the scale of destruction and the plight of civilians through news reports and social media, which prompted an outpouring of support and solidarity.

International reactions to Operation Protective Edge varied, with some countries expressing strong condemnation of Israel's military tactics, while others emphasized the need for a political resolution to the Israeli-Palestinian conflict. These reactions influenced the nature and extent of international aid and reconstruction efforts, as countries aligned themselves with different positions.

Moreover, the legal implications and violations of international law during the military operation raised important questions about accountability and justice. The international community's response to these violations was instrumental in shaping the subsequent aid and reconstruction efforts, as accountability mechanisms were put in place to ensure that assistance reached those in need and helped rebuild Gaza in a just and sustainable manner.

In conclusion, international aid and reconstruction efforts played a vital role in addressing the humanitarian consequences of Operation Protective Edge and rebuilding Gaza. The response from the international community, including governments, organizations, and individuals, was crucial in providing immediate relief and long-term support for the affected population. The lessons learned from these efforts can inform future responses to conflicts and contribute to the quest for a just and lasting resolution to the Israeli-Palestinian conflict.

Chapter 10: Analysis of the Effectiveness of Hamas Rocket Attacks on Israeli Targets

Assessment of Rockets' Range and Accuracy

The assessment of rockets' range and accuracy is a crucial aspect when analyzing the dynamics of Operation Protective Edge, the 2014 Israeli Military Operation in Gaza in response to rocket attacks by Hamas. This subchapter delves into the scientific evaluation of the rockets launched by Hamas, their impact on Israeli targets, and the implications for both sides of the conflict.

Understanding the range and accuracy of these rockets is vital for historians and politicians seeking to comprehend the military strategies employed by both Hamas and the Israeli Defense Forces (IDF) during this operation. By assessing the rockets' capabilities, historians can analyze the tactical decisions made by Hamas, while politicians can evaluate the effectiveness of the IDF's defense measures and the necessity of their military response.

The rockets used by Hamas during Operation Protective Edge varied in range and accuracy. Historians can examine the evolution of these rockets over time and the technological advancements that allowed Hamas to extend their reach and improve their precision. By understanding the limitations and capabilities of these weapons, historians can paint a more accurate picture of the conflict and its impact on the Israeli-Palestinian conflict.

Furthermore, assessing the rockets' range and accuracy allows for an analysis of their impact on Israeli targets. By understanding the potential damage caused by these rockets, politicians can evaluate the threat level posed by Hamas and the necessity of Israel's military response. This assessment also sheds light on the potential humanitarian consequences of these attacks, such as casualties, destruction of infrastructure, and psychological trauma experienced by Israeli civilians.

Additionally, this subchapter explores the long-term implications of Operation Protective Edge on the Israeli-Palestinian conflict. By examining the effectiveness of Hamas' rocket attacks and the countermeasures employed by the IDF, historians and politicians can assess the impact of this military operation on the overall balance of power and the potential for future conflicts.

In conclusion, the assessment of rockets' range and accuracy is a crucial component in understanding the dynamics of Operation Protective Edge. It provides valuable insights for historians and politicians, shedding light on military strategies, humanitarian consequences, and the long-term implications of this conflict on the Israeli-Palestinian relationship. By analyzing these aspects, a comprehensive understanding of Operation Protective Edge can be achieved.

Civilian Casualties and Psychological Impact in Israel

Operation Protective Edge: Unveiling the Israeli Military Response to Rocket Attacks by Hamas

Introduction:

As historians and politicians delve into the intricate details of Operation Protective Edge, it becomes crucial to comprehend the multifaceted impact this military operation had on different stakeholders. While much attention has been given to the humanitarian consequences in Gaza, this subchapter aims to shed light on the civilian casualties and psychological impact experienced by the Israeli population during the conflict. Understanding these aspects is vital for a comprehensive analysis of the operation and its long-term implications on the Israeli-Palestinian conflict.

Civilian Casualties:

Operation Protective Edge saw a significant number of civilian casualties in Israel, primarily due to the indiscriminate rocket attacks launched by Hamas. The rockets targeted densely populated areas, leaving no distinction between military and civilian targets. Historians and politicians need to discern the gravity of these casualties, the lives disrupted, and the trauma inflicted upon the Israeli population.

Psychological Impact:

The psychological impact on Israeli civilians cannot be underestimated. The constant fear of rocket attacks and the need to seek shelter became a part of daily life for millions of Israelis. The psychological toll on children, in particular, was immense, with studies showing increased rates of anxiety, post-traumatic stress disorder, and other psychological disorders. Policymakers must consider these long-lasting effects when formulating strategies for conflict resolution.

International Reactions and Legal Implications:

The international community and legal experts closely observed the Israeli response during Operation Protective Edge.

Understanding the legal implications and potential violations of international law is essential for both historians and politicians. Assessing the proportionality of the Israeli Defense Forces' actions and the measures taken to minimize civilian casualties is critical in determining the overall impact of the operation.

Media Coverage and Propaganda:

The media played a significant role in shaping public opinion during Operation Protective Edge. Understanding the media coverage and potential propaganda is imperative for historians and politicians analyzing the conflict. The examination of media narratives and biases can provide insights into the dissemination of information and its impact on public perception.

Conclusion:

This subchapter provides historians and politicians with a comprehensive understanding of the civilian casualties and psychological impact experienced by Israelis during Operation Protective Edge. By examining these aspects, policymakers can gain insights into the human costs of the conflict and develop strategies that prioritize the protection of civilian lives. Moreover, this analysis contributes to the broader understanding of the long-term consequences and implications of Operation Protective Edge on the Israeli-Palestinian conflict as a whole.

Israeli Defense Measures and Countermeasures

The chapter "Israeli Defense Measures and Countermeasures" delves into the comprehensive military response by the Israeli Defense Forces (IDF) during the 2014 Israeli military operation in Gaza, known as Operation Protective Edge. This subchapter aims to provide a thorough analysis of the strategies, tactics, and measures employed by Israel to counter the relentless rocket attacks launched by Hamas militants.

Operation Protective Edge marked a turning point in the Israeli-Palestinian conflict, with Hamas launching thousands of rockets into Israeli territory, targeting civilian populations indiscriminately. In response, the IDF implemented a multifaceted defense strategy to safeguard its citizens and neutralize the threat posed by Hamas.

The first section of this subchapter explores the various defense measures employed by Israel, including the Iron Dome missile defense system. Historically unprecedented in its effectiveness, the Iron Dome intercepted and destroyed a significant number of incoming rockets, saving countless lives and minimizing the impact of Hamas' attacks. The chapter also analyzes other defensive strategies such as early warning systems, bomb shelters, and the use of civilian safe areas.

Furthermore, the subchapter delves into the countermeasures adopted by the IDF to suppress Hamas' rocket capabilities. It examines the precision airstrikes conducted by the Israeli Air Force to target Hamas infrastructure, rocket launchers, and weapons depots. The use of ground forces to dismantle Hamas tunnels, which served as a critical means of infiltration and weapon smuggling, is also explored.

In addition to the military aspects, this subchapter sheds light on the psychological effects of the operation on civilians living in Gaza. It examines the ethical dilemmas faced by the IDF in striking a balance between protecting its own citizens and minimizing harm to non-combatants in densely populated areas.

Moreover, the legal implications and alleged international law violations during the military operation are analyzed, providing a comprehensive assessment of the IDF's adherence to international norms. The economic impact of Operation Protective Edge on Gaza is also examined, shedding light on the long-term consequences for the Palestinian population.

Lastly, this subchapter addresses the long-term implications of Operation Protective Edge on the Israeli-Palestinian conflict, including the political impact, humanitarian consequences, media coverage, propaganda, and international reactions. It provides historians and politicians with a comprehensive understanding of the multifaceted aspects of this milestone military operation.

Chapter 11: Long-Term Consequences and Implications of Operation Protective Edge on the Israeli-Palestinian Conflict

Shifts in Power Dynamics and Relations

The 2014 Israeli military operation in Gaza, known as Operation Protective Edge, brought about significant shifts in power dynamics and relations in the Israeli-Palestinian conflict. This subchapter aims to delve into the various aspects of these shifts and their implications for both historians and politicians.

Operation Protective Edge marked a turning point in the power dynamics between Israel and Hamas, the militant group controlling Gaza. The Israeli Defense Forces (IDF) showcased their military prowess and technological superiority, employing advanced weaponry and tactics to neutralize Hamas rocket attacks. This display of strength not only tilted the power balance in favor of Israel but also shattered the perception of invincibility that Hamas had cultivated among its supporters.

Furthermore, the operation highlighted the evolving relations between Israel and the international community. While Israel received support from its traditional allies, such as the United States, it also faced condemnation from international organizations and some nations for its alleged violations of international law and human rights. This shift in international relations had profound political implications, forcing Israel to re-evaluate its strategies and consider alternative approaches to garnering international support.

Operation Protective Edge also brought to the forefront the humanitarian consequences of the Israeli military operation. The high civilian casualty rates and destruction of infrastructure in Gaza sparked global outrage and raised questions about the ethics of the Israeli response. Historians and politicians analyzing these humanitarian consequences must critically assess the impact on the civilian population and the long-term ramifications for the Israeli-Palestinian conflict.

Media coverage and propaganda played a crucial role during Operation Protective Edge, shaping public opinion and influencing international reactions. The subchapter will explore the various narratives presented by Israeli and Palestinian media outlets, as well as the challenges faced by journalists reporting from the conflict zone. Understanding the media dynamics during this operation is essential for historians and politicians seeking to grasp the complexities of the Israeli-Palestinian conflict.

In conclusion, Operation Protective Edge brought about significant shifts in power dynamics and relations, impacting not only the military strategies employed by Israel and Hamas but also the perception of both parties on the global stage. By examining the political, humanitarian, and media aspects of this operation, historians and politicians can gain valuable insights into the long-term consequences and implications for the Israeli-Palestinian conflict.

Impact on Peace Process and Negotiations

The 2014 Israeli military operation in Gaza, known as Operation Protective Edge, had a significant impact on the peace process and negotiations between Israel and Palestine. This subchapter aims to examine the various dimensions of this impact, shedding light on the complexities that arose during and after the operation.

Firstly, it is important to acknowledge that Operation Protective Edge further strained the already fragile relationship between Israel and Palestine. The intense military response by the Israeli Defense Forces (IDF) to the rocket attacks by Hamas resulted in a high number of civilian casualties and widespread destruction in Gaza. These humanitarian consequences added to the grievances and resentment felt by the Palestinian population, making it even more challenging to build trust and engage in productive negotiations.

Furthermore, the media coverage and propaganda surrounding Operation Protective Edge played a crucial role in shaping international perceptions of the conflict. Both Israeli and Palestinian sides utilized media outlets to present their narratives and gain support for their respective causes. This manipulation of information further polarized public opinion and hindered diplomatic efforts towards peace.

The international community's reactions to the operation also had a significant impact on the peace process. While some countries condemned Israel's military tactics and called for an immediate ceasefire, others expressed support for Israel's right to defend itself against rocket attacks. These divergent positions complicated the diplomatic landscape and made it difficult to find a common ground for negotiations.

Moreover, the psychological effects on civilians living in Gaza during the operation cannot be overlooked. The constant fear, trauma, and stress experienced by the Palestinian population had long-lasting consequences on their mental well-being. These psychological scars made it even more challenging to foster an environment conducive to peaceful negotiations.

Operation Protective Edge also raised important legal implications and international law violations. The excessive use of force, targeting of civilian infrastructure, and allegations of war crimes by both sides brought attention to the need for accountability and justice. These violations further complicated the peace process and created hurdles for future negotiations.

In conclusion, the impact of Operation Protective Edge on the peace process and negotiations between Israel and Palestine was profound and far-reaching. The humanitarian, psychological, legal, and diplomatic dimensions of this impact need to be thoroughly analyzed and understood to develop effective strategies for conflict resolution. It is vital for historians and politicians to engage in an objective examination of these complexities to pave the way for a peaceful and sustainable resolution to the Israeli-Palestinian conflict.

Prospects for Future Conflict or Resolution

As historians and politicians delve into the complexities of Operation Protective Edge, the 2014 Israeli military operation in Gaza in response to rocket attacks by Hamas, they are confronted with a crucial question: what are the prospects for future conflict or resolution in the Israeli-Palestinian conflict?

The military operation, with its devastating consequences and far-reaching implications, has left an indelible mark on the region. It is imperative to understand the long-term consequences and implications of Operation Protective Edge in order to assess the prospects for future conflict or resolution.

One of the key factors to consider is the political impact of the operation. The Israeli government's decision to launch a large-scale military campaign against Hamas was met with both support and criticism. The operation highlighted the deep political divisions within Israel and the Palestinian territories, making the prospects for future resolution more challenging.

Moreover, the humanitarian consequences of the Israeli military operation cannot be overlooked. The high number of civilian casualties, destruction of infrastructure, and displacement of thousands of Palestinians have further fueled resentment and a sense of injustice. Addressing these humanitarian concerns is crucial for any potential resolution and the prevention of future conflicts.

Media coverage and propaganda during Operation Protective Edge played a significant role in shaping international perceptions. The biased narratives and information warfare employed by both sides further polarized opinions and hindered constructive dialogue. Learning from these media pitfalls can help future negotiations promote a more balanced narrative and facilitate conflict resolution.

The international reactions to Operation Protective Edge were diverse, reflecting the complexities of the Israeli-Palestinian conflict. While some countries condemned the Israeli military response, others expressed support for Israel's right to defend itself. Understanding these international dynamics is essential for assessing the prospects for future conflict or resolution.

Psychological effects on civilians living in Gaza during the operation cannot be underestimated. The trauma and fear experienced by the population, particularly children, have long-lasting consequences. Addressing the psychological impact of conflict is crucial for rebuilding trust and fostering a conducive environment for future resolution.

Another critical aspect to consider is the legal implications and international law violations during the military operation. The alleged human rights abuses and violations of the laws of war have raised questions about accountability and justice. Addressing these legal implications is vital for future conflict prevention and resolution.

Analyzing the military strategy and tactics employed by the Israeli Defense Forces during Operation Protective Edge is essential for understanding the dynamics of conflict. Assessing the effectiveness of Hamas rocket attacks on Israeli targets is equally important. Such analyses can inform future military strategies and countermeasures, potentially reducing the likelihood of future conflicts.

The economic impact of Operation Protective Edge on Gaza has been devastating. The destruction of infrastructure and the blockade on goods and services have further exacerbated the already dire economic conditions. Addressing the economic consequences of the military operation is crucial for future stability and the prospects for conflict resolution.

Finally, the long-term consequences and implications of Operation Protective Edge on the Israeli-Palestinian conflict must be thoroughly examined. Understanding the impact of the operation on political dynamics, public opinion, and regional alliances is crucial for assessing the prospects for future conflict or resolution.

In conclusion, Operation Protective Edge has left a profound impact on the Israeli-Palestinian conflict. The prospects for future conflict or resolution depend on addressing various aspects, including political divisions, humanitarian consequences, media coverage, international reactions, psychological effects, legal implications, military strategies, economic impact, and long-term consequences. By carefully analyzing these factors, historians and politicians can contribute to a deeper understanding of the Israeli-Palestinian conflict and work towards a more peaceful future.